Chronicles of Cosmic Chaos In The Fourth Dimension

poems by
Sophia Falco

UnCollected Press

Cover Art: *Dystopian Vibes, ©Sophia Falco*

Epigraph: *Copyright © 2020 by David Sheff, reprinted by permission of ICM Partners*

Book Design by:

UnCollected Press
8320 Main Street, 2nd Floor
Ellicott City, MD 21043

For more books by UnCollected Press:
www.therawartreview.com

First Edition 2023
ISBN: 979-8-9867243-5-5

*For my younger self, my future self,
and my present self*

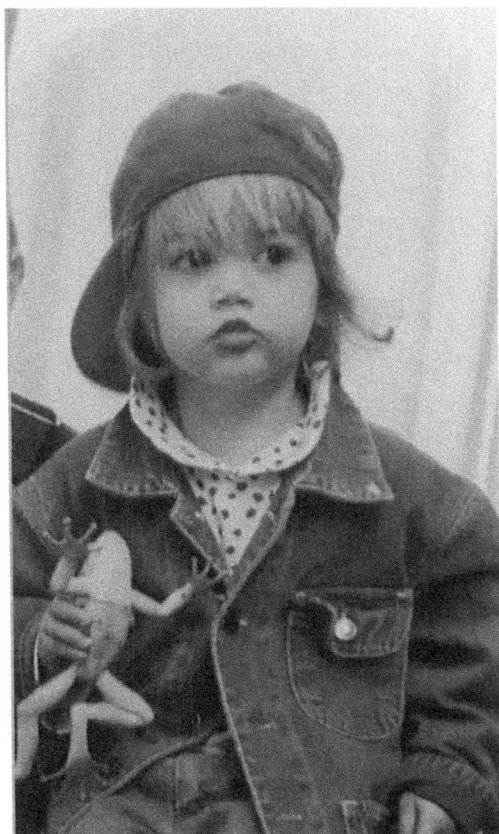

(Sophia, 1997)

TABLE OF CONTENTS

"Hope and fear are two sides of the same coin. Both are traps. But remember how both rob you of the present moment."

The Buddhist On Death Row: How One Man Found Light In The Darkest Place

SO MANY ENDINGS IN ONE PLACE

The end of the incense trail was what I followed,

    that dying scent barely wafted out of her

living room, those hints of sweet lavender

    eventually would falter in her red incense holder

she bought from an art museum used

    countless times now filled with stunted sticks

so many ends built up and up, those ends

    would eventually disintegrate turning ash-like

the dawn of so many endings in one place, and she

    asked me, while her gaze was past my eyes instead

above my head on her two tiny pet birds one bright

    blue and one bright yellow in her rusted bird cage

(chirping countless times) about the final moment of

    that tragedy on how he ended it while I didn't want

to dwell on his end while declaring there are no

    fairytale endings instead too many tragic endings

as she mindlessly continued to buy more,

she didn't think twice about when one burnt out,

she didn't think twice about never emptying the holder

    as a birthday gift she gave me incense sticks

a red matching holder (I never lit one myself)

    this time eucalyptus scented like those trees

near the lake near the place called home, and when

    I returned after her dinner party as the day ended

I became fearful in the dark not because it's hard

    to see, but because I was with my fears, and I

didn't self-harm so I didn't need to end that, but

    was so close oh so close to the beginning.

I. SIDE ONE

BIRDIE HOP

"Birdie Hop" was my first sentence   still yearning to fly I
stretch to my   fullest wingspan visualizing   while the
wind ruffles my black t-shirt like   little feathers   my eyes
are closed   I see black   suddenly I embody a crow
unable   to escape   my feet stuck   to the pavement
attempting   to flap my wings   they buckle   under the
weight of the sorrow   weight of the world
weight of the past   this present moment a Picasso painting
that's more demon   than person   these weird shapes
bending reality   I can still   see the humanity   a fractured
mosaic   of this life   now a fractured wing

NEIGHBORHOOD BUDDHIST WITH ALZHEIMER'S

Not from the heavens, but a sign from above I spotted him
sitting on a wooden bench at the park after reading: *The
Buddhist on Death Row* as he watched on my basketball
taking flight with my right hand to shoot, my left as a guide
on a hot streak completing Around The World.

I felt I was walking on the moon or walking on the sun
wishing for him to be the light to guide me since
still my crossover unable to fake out the demons lurking
(confided my secrets with Hoop) I jinxed myself. Asked the
question, he replied: "Never heard of it."

Then started staring at my basketball once bright color like
the setting sun fading away like my spirit now the grip
worn down no longer can grasp without slipping out of my
hands, therefore this is not always—the teaching of
impermanence.

He whose name started with H or J depending on who was
addressing him. Gave me a choice, invited me to his secret
garden poured soda in a glass with perhaps less soda than
ice. Once they told me smash ice cubes or hold on to them.

I knew this would melt becoming water slipping through
the spaces between my fingers. Pondering the problems of
the world with a grin with a stranger. I called him a week
later, and he could he no long remember my name.

WORLD BACKWARDS

A poet sitting next
to a professional
the purple couch

                located on the
                first floor of a
                two-story house

failed the test of
spelling "world"
backwards

                tripped up
                not tripping
                my memories

swirled together
like that blue green
marble shattered

                now upended
                yes, a method
                to this madness

only one
correct answer
I didn't question

                this word choice,
                I bet he couldn't
                explain why

(standard protocols)
instead of
researching

                its history, to Google
                "death" or "die"
                blocked.

HEARTS

The shaking of the hands
      the shaking of the arms
           the shaking of the body
    my hands
  my arms
my body,
   but all
       do not feel like mine anymore.

To repeat the phrase aloud: "This is me."
while touching my heart was what they
advised me to do in hopes for me to
feel grounded once again, but no
this entity is touching my red shirt
that covers my chest that covers the
heartspace yes, there's a space for
my heart, but this space stretches
for too long, empty.

BE HERE NOW

Handmade sketches on colorful printer paper
with life-affirming notes lined up in a row above
the cheap wooden headboards these beds like
musical chairs individuals coming going haunted by
their own minds intertwined with demons prowling
of all ages jumbled up like an owl's pellet with tiny
remnants of bird bones while the inside of these pillows
not composed of feathers—that one sketch of a
tortured sun with charcoal eyes reminiscent of a face
that died staring burned an image in the back of my
head when our eyes locked each night. I told her she
who hears voices to take it down even though it declared:
Be Here Now such uplifting messages yet I wondered
about the anonymous artist: maybe gone or maybe long
gone or maybe reincarnated as an owl soaring overhead,
if the artist believed them or it was just a façade to
get out of here and if innocence could come back again.

NOT AN ODE TO A BUCKET HAT

A bucket hat in the pattern of *Starry Night*
the hero Vincent Van Gogh who deserves
a purple heart yet him wearing that hat
talking of telepathy in a mental institution
playing the piano, claiming he's: "Gonna
blow up musically to become a star!" like
the color of the yellow brick road, he
said his piss smelled like bananas (to
make banana bread, to make a banana
smoothie, to eat a banana and all of this
he didn't do) took a pill to create this
scent like a banana like the color of
his urine, and dubstep, stepping over
my boundaries not wanting to know
what is going through his mind unearthed
from reality looking at me with those
possessed eyes under a starless sky.

REMNANTS OF RASPBERRIES

Remnants of pink lip balm on her left ear
from the woman who took care of her in her
remaining years, you cannot wait for some
special being to drink the life force when the
time is up in this physical realm too much to
take for this furry creature cannot carry her own
meager weight her life has past fulfilled the glass
that was never half empty, but her inquisitive
eyes saw too much sorrow, too much heartache,
too much fear, but never crushed her spirits, and
she couldn't hear "I love you." as I exited the
empty space of that doorway housing the raspberry
door with a brittle windowpane.

HOT AIR BALLOON CORN MAZE

Those corn husks littered the entrance to the maze that
were tossed about like abandoned ragdoll toys that fell out
of each child's stroller continuously as they exited.

When I entered, all I could see was green with yellow
unable to witness this hot air balloon shape from within,
but instead I would have had to take to the skies.

Trying to fly away, I made it to the basket as the wind
rustled the remaining leaves as the crows started
returning to play with the corn husks and ragdoll toys
as the night started to fall.

Promising light blue vanished from above, and a pointless
imprint was left in the dirt while the farmer's dog was
running about in a superman costume, and I couldn't help
think of her who once was.

Roxie, my dog the adventurer, who would find her way into
the white plastic laundry basket with many square cut-outs
(to peek out of) tucked away in the closet—once on her
own makeshift hot air balloon without the red balloon.

SPIDER LEGS
after Tommy Orange

I would pluck the
daddy long-legs
from the peeling
    yellow painted
    walls placing them
    in my doll house
        out of rubber bands
        bedazzled with glitter
        I created tiny leashes
            every morning for 223
            days I walked my spiders
            down the miniature flight
                of stairs eventually
                taping them down
                before their escape
                    Spiders want me
                    specifically in this
                    two-story house
              biting my legs at night
              became infected with
              pus coming out
            the four red circles
            no one else afflicted
            a trap and a home
        spider silk can be
        broken by the wind
        grief consumes my
      body these bites
      treated painless
      not my psyche
    to embark for the
    journey of acceptance

this staircase does
not lead me
towards the light
instead into the dark
basement covered
in cobwebs the answer
lies in a web—a tree
is not the right
metaphor I must
now free myself
from the silky
strands that are
shielding my eyes
from being
wide-open.

TRYING TO LET GO

The leaves are going downwards
I am falling into darkness,
the breaking of a heart

                   to be clear, my heart, and what does
                       it means when a dried crinkled
                         maroon leaf gets stepped on?

Stepped on by an unsuspecting
shoe, and then breaks apart
into tiny fragments, and

                     I try to forget by mindfully
                 watching the leaves fall until
                         there are none left.

FOOTSTEPS

Carrying my flip-flops by the straps in my
left hand after walking miles in them, a bad
blister on the top of my right foot, now barefoot
on the sidewalk the hot concrete hurting my feet
all while getting stared at by passing pedestrians.

I landed on a bus bench with my shaking
hands clasped tight pressing against my
forehead my arms each at a 45° angle sobbing
with my eyes closed then hearing a voice
come closer: "Are you OK?"

If the number of footsteps already taken
could speak: 10,000 steps of not OK, going
up a dirt trail tripping over roots, the sky did
not fall whereas I, falling like a shooting star,
then being questioned not the star of my own life.

Not even a supporting role, but a nobody in fact,
worse than a nobody, a burden, an invisible
adverse reaction, then terror: an authority male
boosting his presence: "We all have bad days,
including me." wanting more information.

This was much more than a bad day. Being
stuck in bed gripping my pillow for hours to
stop shaking, barely able to get out of the bed to
get water—so many thoughts colliding at once
like the explosion of a supernova.

A 'courtesy call', however the courtesy call
would have been to leave me alone instead of
intimidation. I refused to give my address, instead

he dropped off me at the post office parking lot
all to show off to his friend at my expense.

My premonition, that our coordinates would
collide—I knew a cop would find me,
me out of everyone in that exact moment in
time of my distress my tears violently bursting.

Good cop or bad cop?

Pained me to run into him at the Fourth
of July party at the local park, hoping he
would not stop to talk to me, but of course, he
did boosting his presence yet again in front
of the same friend while I wanted to yell:

NO, WE ALL DON'T JUST HAVE BAD DAYS!

BEYOND THE BEYOND

He resurfaced as I was
drowning at the park, dragging
me down further on such a pristine
day: children running about, playing hide
-and-seek, laughing, groomed dogs barking,
chasing muddy tennis balls and some not muddy

yet I tried to seek
refuge away by sobbing
on another different bench still
on land, but haven't landed in the
present while the memory of him not
to close to home because home is undefined to
me, and I thought what if I don't make it too, haunted

by his absence of
presence, across the other
side lies the beyond not a pond,
currently I am barely above the currents,
swirling are the whirlpools, blurring of the
now, the future much more than a distant dream,
the past raging like the river, those nightmares burst

that dam of self-preservation,
a reservation, reserved, to serve, no,
I've never served on a battle field, but
these demons in my mind lurk and become
bigger eating the present, and I look in the mirror
not knowing who I am, I am who I am and she doesn't

like it! I just want an outstretched hand to grasp, and dialed

the phone to reach
my rock all alone in the
park, this mood bigger than the
horizon, to rise like the sun to rise from
bed instead of stuck stuck stuck acting like
I was five trying not to die repeating: "I don't know",
really I knew, but there were no words in my vocabulary
to describe that immense pain, the flooding of memories

to roll the dice, the
cards were dealt not revealing
my opinion on them yet trying to
break this cycle; I will not be another
who falls, the falling of leaves, changing of
the season, to change to be the person I am meant to be.

HAIKU TRAIN: RAILWAYS 1

starlit sky does not
equate to lit torches fire
still seeing darkness

two syllables said
"bipolar" scared me for my
future still here now

blue often ocean
remaining constant beauty
force in my life still

notes not notes music
the soundtrack of life silent
tears remain at will

rectangular route
I called you barely holding
the fort down, my soul

mind not united
yet bipolar doesn't have to
be a death sentence

THE FIRST TIME

the world was fake,
merely a blue green marble
that started to crack, the lines
ran too deep the same day it rolled
off the kitchen table after the argument that
this marble was more than just a marble also a
representation of the ocean and the continents, but his
facts stood as he blocked the door way: "Just two colors."

I became as small
as the marble as the four walls
started to close in on me, shrinking
as I buried my face in these hands that were
no longer mine alone in my bedroom, feeling like
the only human in the world—"It just feels as if you're
dying, take the medication, and go to bed." I complied

after hanging up the
phone after having yelled:
"I'M DYING" in a safe town then
judging myself by myself wondering
the lasting mental image of the blue green marble,
it was just a marble the first time I saw it, I am
just a human when I look in the mirror they say there's still

the potential for
it to be a marble once again
to create a mosaic, a new narrative yet
I know never the same, the shards, I'm still
reaching for the missing glue, unequipped to be the
savior of this world fearing the arrival of the second time.

CIRCULARITY

I was not in a movie, but instead in a moving car;
point A to point B missing the point on my way to
the Haunted House for another stay, dejected, and
those once rejected tears came rolling down.

Still silently as she was the one at the wheel as
I was the passenger as I broke down, and unfolded
the paper origami crane nestled in my jean
pocket now reverted to just a single sheet.

Of white paper, purposefully problematically
unpragmatically while the monstrous crane by
the side of the road stayed motionless, I didn't
want to get out of the vehicle.

Because this road had too many forks in it, and
as I arrived I was served dinner with only a
single silver spoon staring at the meal prepared
unprepared for round two.

CONFINED MOVEMENTS

Sneaking green tea
bags from the oversized
box of 100 located in
the lowest left-hand
drawer, I tucked this
in the way back to
try to hide it from
the rest technically
still keeping it in the
tea drawer located
next to the oven across
from the kitchen sink,
forbidden were energy
drinks along with the
dishwasher detergent
locked up in a tall,
black metal cabinet
in a two-story house.

When I arrived, I
barely spoke whereas
the countless cups
of green tea did hot
water splashed when
hitting the bottom
of various mugs as
I hit rock bottom as
I poured the hot
water from their
cooler in secrecy,
not revealing how
many cups per day.

In secrecy, the only
place was the
bathroom to think
of something nice
so I locked the door to
visualize beautiful
women yet not for
too long 22 minutes
max checking the
time as not to have
suspicion arise.

Outside that door
chaos ensued as one
individual was
hospitalized taken
away in an
ambulance—
I saw my past
come back to life
in that very moment.

Moments. Hours
spent with the trusty
basketball hoop that
did not require me
talking instead it
talked back to me
(when they finally
got a net) with
swishes, not wishes.

They wished for me
instead to color in
the patterns of empty
hearts, but no pencils

could cheer me up
even though I had
more than the
rainbow at hand.

Hands. He who
made Greek food.
I who messed up
the chicken dinner.
Them monitoring
my bowel movements.
My roommate, too.
Rooms. Sharing
one conflicts.

I who was writing
relentlessly. Karaoke.
Nightshifts.
Flashlights
got shined in
my eyes. To see
if you're okay,
okay enough.

FRUIT CUP

I wanted to crush the fruit in that tiny
white, paper cup lined with plastic to
witness the juices ooze and flow out
in different colors from the raspberry
oh so red, the miniscule piece of
lemon oh so yellow, the blackberry
oh so purple (the juice, after each
bite, stained her shirt that was white,
almost resembling drops of blood the
last thing I wanted to be reminded
of as she mindlessly continued to pop
more one by one into her mouth eating
those shiny blackberries straight from
the green plastic container not even
washed until she felt obliged to offer
me one: "Do you want a blackberry?"
I politely declined while she was
too busy to hear me instead admiring
the blue sky and white fluffy clouds
passing by lost in make believes too
oblivious to recognize my intense gaze
off far in the distance at the smoke
bellowing from the stacks mirroring
the fear rising within my being all
to avoid looking at her shirt) a
supposed mindfulness exercise 22
minutes examining and tasting; a
bunch of disturbed people sitting in
a circle as if fruit is the key, and for
them it was, and that left me laughing.

RIVERS

Those blue veins closer to the surface, the
tributaries of the channel—this is not a
tribute poem channeling into an obituary the
only one who was absent from her funeral.

AGING TEDDY BEAR IN GRIEF

The 20 something year old in 2022
clutched his oversized aging
teddy bear as he was singing
along too loudly in the oversized
white van to Journey's lyrics: *Don't
stop believing.* All I wanted
was this to just stop as believing
in myself diminished as we passed
all subsequent green traffic lights.
(We grieved together in grief group.)
Then back to the white van yet
again, but stuck on the return
route with other lyrics going *I'm
missing you more than you know*
followed by *I won't let you go*
as we hit all the red traffic lights.

TRAPPED LIGHT

Those lovely fireflies are prisoners in a
glass jar on her kitchen table, their trapped
light on display like the diminishing light
within my being. I would love to free them.
The only way to release them I pondered,
was to smash the jar. (The lid has rusted
shut on this antique mason jar.)

Then shards of glass would be flying about, and
they would be endangered even more—it is not
worth the risk to do so yet at the same time, I
don't want to witness these fireflies dying. Dwindling
is my spirit needing to shake it out like
wet t-shirts prior to being hung up with
wooden clips on the clothesline.

Even the radiant sun has not given me
warmth unable to thaw out of this darkness;
still hibernating. If only my spirit could
drink the sun's rays. Radiating through
the glass, the light was dimmer the next night.
The owner of these lovely fireflies declared:
"Fake it till you make it."

Yet they are not faking it till they make it,
instead they are just being, but trapped. Their
authenticity needs to be freed, and with agency,
I declared I would be the rescuer whereas I
cannot seem to rescue myself.

I found the way to rescue the fireflies,
if there's a will there's a way they say, by
putting the jar under a stream of warm water.

(If only my stream of consciousness
was pleasant.) I scrubbed the edges of
the lid with a small wire brush, and opened
this outside freedom for the light. If only
it was that easy to free the light within.

BACKWARDS LOVE

Knowing the correct answer yet not
knowing what love is as this word rings
hollow as sorrow stole its spot, a mark in
time these rings of a tree can only be seen
when cut, and I cannot stop thinking about
scratches, to just scratch the surface my purpose,
I don't even love myself as I'm far removed in
another galaxy, and I wish when I thought of the
word love it wouldn't cause me to shake
with fear and well up with tears.

WHILE WATER SLIPS THROUGH MY FINGERS

They say the color of the water is that of black tea in the deepest river, and what mirrored this was my sorrow all that depth compressed in this body of mine, my body, let's just say sorrow resided in my bones something tangible.

I then saw in white and black, but she told me this world is still in bright hues yet all of those have bled out in front of me into a sticky black puddle like hot tar. My strange shoes now making footprints to be perhaps permanent on this road lined with colorless trees having uprooted the old asphalt while the roses followed suit, and even the sky, just empty space. She loved to wear gray whereas I didn't feel her love yet I missed her, like how I missed the feeling opposite to sorrow.

Her favorite idiom: "The weight of the world is on my shoulders." repeated so many times that those words spun around in my mind like earth itself. In secrecy, it was I who held up the world, that minuscule marble the only object that presented itself to me in colors I found neglected on the side of the newly tarred road.

Holding the glass sphere between my left thumb and index finger, I aligned it up to the sun to witness the blue and green sparkling. The weight of the world finally off my shoulders, but just a mirage manifesting in this marble that was surprisingly heavy and then threw it out while I felt she was through with me—

"I just don't understand your poetry." translating to she just doesn't understand me. I came to the conclusion that living there was just a house not a home. Just me in my own corner without boxing gloves. Just me in my own corner in the ring trying to escape, but still dependent like how the rose needs the sun. The little prince needs his rose and I need the sun (that still rises) even those light beams bouncing, I could see them more clearly when they filtered in through the window illuminating dust.

Her rose petals recently turned to dust. If only sorrow could turn to dust and disintegrate, rubbing it between my fingers like ash to watch the wind carry it away. I discovered what I would like, for someone to be close to me, at night I wish they would just hold my hand, hold me close to tell me:

This is not your fault, and *I love you,*
while my eyes are blurry with tears:
You will be okay—more than just okay.

SPECTATOR

The era of simplicity no longer
stands as I am in the stands
merely a spectator watching
myself dressed and undressed.

                    Trying to decipher in the mirror
                    if I somewhat resemble a man;
                    wearing my flannel deemed
                    "lumberjack shirt" as a joke.

As a power move, but owning
no dresses, and as I dress myself,
I think maybe my face; yet I
don't want to admit confusion.

                    But when my gender gets
                    questioned, the dominos fall,
                    the past falls backwards, not spring
                    forwards, never feminine enough.

Yet feeling powerless. I would
rather have the power a man does, but
would never want to be one while
women are so beautiful; their breasts.

                    My breasts, wishing to consensually
                    touch another woman's breasts
                    whereas my chest holds fear, too
                    my lungs less air as anxiety rises.

I dislike mirrors. I hate seeing
myself in photographs, and as I
stand there, there is more than
the physical, but distance.

32

                    Upon distance guarded upon
                guarded. The shield was too fierce
                  it cracked under its own weight.
                     This body feels too heavy.

While this mind is trying to
withstand the test of time or the
wall. There's a mirror, mirrors are
man-made, and I didn't make it a point.

                     To ponder the binaries the blurring
                  the defining. The undefining when all
                  I want is to embody a woman, and be
                  with a woman saluting and unsaluting.

The mirror—*check yourself before you
wreck yourself* a man would say versus
the *lemon test,* however the test lies
before my very own eyes.

SNAPSHOTS

I solemnly refuted this is not fair; the
turning of a Ferris Wheel, oh he loved
candy, and isn't it dandy this pretending
of a pretentious happiness. Frivolous.

Falsified, fairy floss not caressing sugar
sticky spaces between my fingers,
granules, blue fingerprints on a white tube—
it wasn't a blue cloud as you claimed.

That would defeat the purpose of a
cloud while I'm way below cloud nine
(invisibility) as I snapped the cardboard
in half as I snapped back:

*"Don't use those nonsensical metaphors
when I can make them better than you!"*
But you proceeded pressing the button
for the cotton candy machine, anyways.

I did not point up above to the cloud
in the shape of an eyeless dog, but as I
held this leash in my right hand that
could have attached to a collar.

No longer with no body to put on;
nobody is listening, but the turning
of time. The brittle cloud wallpaper
starting to get undone on the edges.

With sheer white now yellowing
bright blue fading away, materials
thinner thus disintegrating yet

those toy clowns were dressed in dresses.

Ageless witnesses on the white wicker
dresser timeless as time ran out as the
wicked color of the wall was revealed
as I peeled the paper away.

HER NOT HIM

Too many times pretending, checking
if midnight came, if a (holographic)
knight in shining armor was to have come
rescue me in 2019 whereas I'd rather have
(in the flesh) a hot woman greet me just
out of the hot shower like in the movie
Like Water for Chocolate assigned
for Spanish class—I saved the
exact time in order to replay
in my dorm room alone (while
most of the guy ballers were impressed
with my shot) instead wishing for a
modern twist with: no blue towel,
her power, her chest, her soft breasts
   yet this opportunity never has arisen,
instead feeling sick to my stomach too often.

TIGER FOR THE NTH TIME

Those twelve numbers got loose escaping
the clock glass like tigers from a cage, still
they are not timeless. A stuffed toy tiger
purchased at a grocery store sits on my bedside
table nameless matching my pink blanket
decorated in patterns of friendly tigers.

In the realm of dreamland he, with black beady
eyes glazed over, could not put his paw up
to summon that tidal wave to stop mid-air
to retreat like his prey. I don't pray, ashamed
I use my hands another way prior to drifting off
to sleep still woke up gasping for air.

As if I was drowning at the beach, my bed
not a lifeboat as tears escaped as I clutched
my blanket tighter as I proceeded to wet
the bed in this 27-year old body (still
in my bright blue basketball shorts) but
no tiger was chasing me even though she
liked to use that analogy for my body.

The physiology: fight or freeze or flight; I
told her I'd rather be a bird for a day to fly
away from here yet still would be caged in
by my own mind no matter how many tigers
looking up I witnessed those clock numbers
replaced by twelve pictures of tigers.

TIMELY OR TIMELESS

Having written countless poems, knowing the truth
that there are actually good or bad poems despite the smile
there is a difference, and no matter my efforts, I cannot
hold my own hand throughout the night.

Instead, I wish I could hide them from myself, but at the
same time I do have two hands blessed to write these words
while they speak of beautiful angels, no, I see angels
without wings that the demons ate, and subsequently them
wounded.

They are freefalling like me into an abyss feeling worthless
still trying to believe in purpose just wanting to reach *okay*
not even the sublime, this time.

The creature with four legs who used to look at me with
sparkling eyes knowing when mine were heavy and full of
sorrow she is nowhere near and there is nowhere to release
my tears, the years are catching up to me.

I was caught in a gigantic spider web full of thorns, cutting
my skin and I cannot cut out of the suffering from my life,
removed, wishing, but the eraser broke: the pencil a stub,
no more words left to be born or liberated, and the thing I
believe in the most is not working nothing is working.

I close my eyes at night still see the sun blinded by the
same rhymes same mantras "this too shall pass"—no and
no I refute again no, more than a decade later counting
down the minutes, counting down the seconds.

Sick of meds not working yet, sick of the broken compass,
sick of the needle, sick of faltering—*The Fault In Our*

Stars they say, and well I say: I am shooting star, and there is no handbook on how to revive a shooting star.

PLAUSIBLE PLANETARIUM

"The ocean and outer space swapped places. Size is not a factor here. Proportions the same. To prevent our earth from getting knocked out of orbit."

That of dystopian delight or utopian unraveling, this worldly-wise tour guide, aware the laws of gravity were suspended still shouted out, with a far too long wink, knowing I could see past her enlightened enigmatic eyes as the truth went awry:

LOVE POEM WITH PURPLE PENS & BLEEDING HEARTS OF INK DRIPPING
after Stephanie Burt

I always text purple heart emojis not red ones afraid of
love even though this is composed of blue and red so
stemming from the same source gravity towards, but
against war yet—feeling wounded my closest friends
know to send a purple heart; an act of bravery of boldness
of beholding, and of being recognized for this struggle
whereas my mother figure sends me red hearts while
I send her my art, but I, still feeling undeserving, (and
wonder why she cares so much) wrote my poems
dedicated to her in purple ink; high quality gel pen as
to not bleed through the page in this world full of hurt,
red reminiscent of blood, and I cannot send a
red heart to this day, but hopefully soon
I will be able to first, like myself
then love myself. Then I will feel deserving
of a Love Poem.

NO NEED FOR A TITLE

Riding on a shooting star to escape
the gravity resistant monstrous dove
with fangs flying across the night
sky in a suit that is resistant to heat.

As this star starts to burn up, I have
my trusty backpack with my trusty
neon orange parachute, I clicked the
red button as I'm going downwards
or down words talking down to the
nurse in the children's psych ward.

Then resuming towards the ocean
somersaulting sky I got hung up in a
baobab tree, but with my trusty pair
of scissors that sometimes I would hide
from myself, I cut it.

I fell on my own two feet upright
(not on all fours nor with three)
traversing in the desert encountering
the little prince, but unable to get
momentum upwards back into
outer space where I needed to be.

This backpack also had a vacuum-
cleaner attached to suck up my
nightmares, suddenly a haunted
hot-air balloon landed and I
hopped aboard to rise back up.

The sky, I emptied the collecting
(opaque) bag with the green button

to deposit my nightmares into a
black hole eating them up whereas
the entire time I was sitting on that
plastic chair with a blue seat at
the lunch table.

Matter of fact, consuming a
Christmas cookie cut out in the
shape of the dove with the real
world that started to crash down
on my shoulders.

I was feeling powerless, I threw out
that half-eaten representation of
flight made, and instead
I asked for sour candies.

HAIKU TRAIN: RAILWAYS 2

love is banned substance
myself gone missing since birth
trying to reclaim

I still have image
of myself microscopic
unlike grand redwood

too much talk of light
candle, prayers no enough to
revive the dead now

to be me not what
she wanted me to turn out
I'm out already

outside the box there
was none to begin with that
I declared today

syllables sounding
when almost in disbelief
keep believing in

WHEN SORROW STRETCHES ACROSS TOO MANY DAYS

These letters cannot spell what has been cast on me to that magnitude, they ask: "Where do you feel this in your body?" and with each breath my chest feels heavier these legs those stairs too much. I'm scared to write to you directly, to call you by your name sorrow—you swallow hope, no it is not "a thing with feathers" even though sometimes I want to be a bird for a day. Today I just want to fly away from here, but even a bird has a heart.

My heart yes, it's too heavy for this body weighing it down with every step as I address these letters to you while I try to silence and rid of your seemingly everlasting presence yet I cannot blame you as I'm watching a crow outside my windowsill with no home to return to.

Resting on the branch of a weeping willow tree, and you live within the rings of these branches while someone wanted to prove the existence of sorrow under a microscope claiming he never experienced sorrow in his life, but I intervened and put up a sign on the weeping willow tree before he approached it that read: "Do Not Touch".

He wanted to cut a branch to supposedly bring you forth sorrow, to supposedly come to the surface to be visible, and to supposedly become tangible whereas this wouldn't have been true, and instead just zapping your lifeforce to bleeding sap.

When understanding of me feels almost nonexistent like how I often feel invisible, and they cannot see this sorrow touching me, hiding in my heart and taking up residency for far too long like those rings a mark in time.

45

II. SIDE TWO

LITTLE HAND AND BIG HAND
for Maya
after Kaveh Akbar

The little hand. The big hand.
Both in reverse. Wish for more time.
He claimed the clock is ticking.
Ticking now backwards.
His claim. This buys more time.
I didn't check. That clock.
Thrown off equilibrium.
Less time equates to heartache.
Her hand is the little hand.
My hand is the bigger hand.
This mother figure. Real.
Almost all knowing.
To sit across from me in silence.
Her presence fills up the room.
Echoes of love.
When despair comes.
She loves me for me.
"Love" never said aloud.
This fear. To leave soon.
Try to avoid. Writing about hands.
Mine are missing something.
I cannot grasp onto emptiness.
Instead I hold onto bag handles.
Miniature unlit candles.
My paper airplanes.
Made from memory.
Not holding space.
For the existence of heaven.
My purple pen.
Holding. Holding.
Holding. Holding.

Cannot catch time that flies.
During daytime. Yet nights.
Too long. Too lonely.
Wake up with jolts.
Glancing at the digital clock.
Seeing red. Not wanting to.
Hope it is morning. It's not.
Hauntings.
I cannot face the past head on.
The face of the grandfather clock.
Too old. The glass cracked.
No longer can protect.
Its own hands.

MOTHERLY

She who acted motherly. She who took my hand.
She who made me chamomile tea. How I wish
she was next to me. To hold my hand, to make
me chamomile tea, she who acted motherly.

Today my hand does not have another hand to
grasp—just empty space. Today I must muster
up the strength to get off my bed to microwave
the lukewarm water in that mug. A chipped
white mug to steep the chamomile tea.

First, I will have to unwrap that minuscule
plastic bag that garnered dust on its fragile
edges slowly with my cold hands, and with
my cold slender fingers. The clock is ticking.

This loss blooming from multiple sources
like a wounded cluster of chamomile flowers.
The clock keeps ticking. A countdown. Yes, I
am still breathing whereas when I'm crying
silently the breath that I claim as my own
gets distorted as if bouncing about in
a house of mirrors.

Zigzagging, illusive, and unpredictable, I'm
unable to catch it like how I'm unable to catch
a shooting star yet tonight a star is shining.
I hope it is shining for me. Can't you see?
I want that light. Instead, I'm back to myself.

I must muster up the strength in this lonely battle.
What's remaining is my paper, and my purple pen.
This pen writes what it wants, wanting her back.

She who acted motherly. She who took my hand.
She who made me chamomile tea. How I wish
she was next to me. To hold my hand, to make
me chamomile tea, she who acted motherly.

WITHOUT HONEY

We never talked about bees,
instead beauty, and the time
we had together was beautiful.

You gave me tea without honey
knowing bees had danced
across those white flowers.

Now when I drink chamomile tea,
I think of you, and if someone
were to ask: "With honey?"

I would politely
shake my head
as to say no.

DEGREES OF SEPARATION

the foot
 the purple sock
  the strange shoe
   the thin black rubber
    the concrete
     the dirt
      the's that
        continue downwards

Alienated was the mind from the body yet at the same time
I knew my brain was telling my foot *move* on my way to
my grandmother's home that hot November afternoon. My
heavy legs were wavering while walking without having
drank—perhaps the passing dog walker thought otherwise
as they crossed the street without making eye contact.

I stumbled to her front door with the doormat in all capital
letters: WELCOME HOME to her house built with too
many rooms. My body was moving about those spaces until
I reached the Kalamata Room; her favorite. (I already knew
before she explained to me that kalamata is the name for
those fancy Greek olives.) I sat down in an antique chair.

I tried to complete her crossword puzzle she barely started
in *The New York Times* she put aside on the side table
neglected with only a few words etched in faint pencil. Not
knowing what was needed to be known, I stared at the deep
purple painted walls instead of completing it, those clues
left me clueless, stood up exited to enter the living room.

My grandmother was moved there permanently during both
the days and nights residing on her hospital bed she was
given. She who looked at me seemingly with a deliberate

yet inquisitive gaze for a minute speechless maybe my face
mask through her off, but then again, sometimes I'm not
even sure of who I am and returned to the Kalamata Room.

As time passed as time stood still, I returned to see if she
was still here with us, she looked up. With the limited
words she had left declared: "Life is short." as she said
each syllable slowly and sorrowfully, her eyes were as keen
as a hawk for those four seconds as this 97-year-old
was approaching something else.

FACE OF THE SUN

A face that died with charcoal eyes
reminded me of her who recently took her
last breath and left this plane of existence
while this sketch is on bright orange paper
that of a tortured sun by an unknown artist
radiating pain from its spot on the
wall across from my bed.

On her deathbed, she was cared for by
my mother recalling every detail about just
prior to the end about playing her favorite
music; Frank Sinatra, about giving her
massages, about feeding her spoonful by
spoonful Oreo ice-cream while I am left alone.

Instead I face the blame, and with
nothing left to say, I sketched a new sun
the other day on white paper. It looked
normal in yellow marker with squiggles
for rays, but these are beyond normal
circumstances anyways so I told
she who hears voices to take it down.

Prior it was as if I was starting at death in
the face each night with the phrase written
in blue floating above its charcoal eyes:
Be Here Now whereas death already arrived
not just in time, but now, and I don't want to
dwell on the colorful cars going to the burial
site like a sorrowful parade on a rainy day.

A TRIP TO JOLENE'S

Purple flashing lights
dots filtering through
the water glass glowing
like my desire to touch
sitting in a room with
each wall covered in
countless pictures
surrounding me still
while the world inside
this microcosm of feels
is spinning to the beat of
this music loud echoes
like my heart beating
tapping my foot wanting
more for these topless
women to come to life
still to this day reaching.

54

TOYS

If it was not considered a toy, that
kaleidoscope—the scope of my sinking
spirits knowing they don't want to fight
for me—I wouldn't have twirled the
homemade (do it yourself) aimlessly.

Those ever-changing patterns predictable, but
simultaneously trying to step out trying
to break free of those deceivingly beautiful
sequences not sequins even though the
toilet paper roll was painted and covered in them.

The foundation of something that once
was complete, but the paper gone just the
roll, rolling down the hill in the freshly-
cut grass creating a hole on my jean that
once covered my knee, and my body
his body, their bodies yet no one is listening
to discuss anything.

The stethoscope the absent-minded doctor
used, well those were my sacred breaths,
my sounds quickening like beating of that drum
the drummer had to fix, tightened that
dry material prior for the placement, and
my tight shoulders then to my ears still
having heard too much.

Wearing pink earplugs to bed, but I cannot block
out these urges, still hearing ringing and
scratches here and there told the doctor I fell
off my bike whereas I don't own a bike, but
even if I had one, I'd riding in rectangles

to an unknown destination.

This house haunted does not equate to a
haunted house, and they're too busy
minding their own business to see me,
see my suffering, see into their pasts.

No magic eight ball here, but they are
equipped with the tarot cards, and I
am the one with too many decks.

CLAWS

Claw marks in the sand towards the
rainbow-colored pond, timidly the
tortoise tries to dip his feet in the
orange, but that means he must pass
the color red which he despises.

Red reminiscent of blood—that
diagonal scar a reminder of that
twig jutting out from the brambles
cutting the side of his abdomen
though he'd prefer if he was the one
with autonomy who did it himself.

A twisted move it would have
been like the ivy suffocating
the dandelion flower. Yellow sun
now fading to gray soon to turn to
dust like the dust that covered
up his claw marks.

He couldn't get past red. He
couldn't get to the blue where
he wanted to wallow in his sorrows
to submerge in them only to
pop back up like how his claws
pop the little bubbles the
sand makes sometimes.

Somewhere past the rainbow
-colored pond lies the unknown.
Over the rainbow. Not clear-cut.
He already feels lost in his mind.
His brain unlike mush. His brain

unlike mud however, like his brain
caught fire, and how to extinguish
those flames are unknown even when
water engulfs his body.

Mind, body; separate.

There is no twine to stitch them back
together. Togetherness is as lost
as that fractured leaf that drifted
out of sight. That drifted past his
naked eye into a land far far away.

He is here, but the time is not now—
it's something else. Elsewhere he is.
Not on this island.

In a pond surrounded by land
then surrounded by more water,
and it's starting to rain. The
concept of an umbrella is inept
yet the last traveler to this island
left one behind.

This became his shelter, but soon
the wind swept it away, and turned it
inside out unlike how he wears
his heart on his sleeve.

COULD HAVE

I'm not asking for prayers, but
easily I could have, but the
world is churning, burning,
I'm still unable to love
myself as they repeat for me to
do so, a broken spirit, I love
poetry more than anything
because my devastatingly
beautiful poems are composed
of carefully chosen words,
combination of letters in those
specific orders, punctuation here
and there my poems fly free at
my will, those killed too much
to bear, to bear arms, let's face it—
prayers will not take the guns
away yet many things are
out of my hands, and still I'm
not asking for prayers, but
easily I could have, but the
world is churning and burning.

GENTLE GEESE
after Mary Oliver

Breaking the surface of my skin.
Like how those geese break the stillness
of the water with their webbed feet.
Whereas it was my own sharp nail from
   my own finger.
Attached to my own right hand now pinkish lines.
Streaked across my left forearm the end of a shooting star.
Unable to foreshadow this point in time
that arrived too quickly,
if I start running in my trusty blue
basketball shorts matching jacket *FLY* stitched in
bold white letters, these lines won't just disappear.
Even under the shade of the weeping
willow tree, they would not notice yet
this harm would still be present—
a wise person of nature yet no longer
wise no longer living
up to this name.

FLYING KNEE

If in the ring, would I be
be the ropes or be the gloves
or be the fighter?

I caught a glimpse of the replay
regarding the historical flying knee
knockout in five seconds while
washing the dishes.

Whereas this blow to my psyche, it
dawned on me while using the liquid
blue dish soap of the same name, but
not in past tense—I used too much;
should have had my ducks in a row.

      Miniature soap bubbles drifting upwards.

Only seeing half of my reflection then
I had a recollection of them wanting me
to be down on my knees to pray, but
instead I hurled those stones at the stained-
glass windows, and heard moans of tortured souls.

(I am trying to have my soul be OK with
just being, and not the recipient of a KO.)

AFTER THE STEPS
after Diane Di Prima

Go to the pharmacy
buy a month's worth supply of Band-Aids
for your blister
buy antibiotic ointment
change the Band-Aid and dress
the wound daily
will take roughly the time span of a
menstrual cycle to heal
hope for no scar so not to
be reminded of that fateful
day full of flaws.

MY BENCH

I wasn't benched, but it was my bench even
with a memorial plaque for someone else
adorned with a bouquet of flowers tied with
green twine on the fragile stems each week.

But I would beat them to it everyday and to
this day claim it's mine. I now have a bird's-eye
view of me there alone trying to cry because there
wasn't space for allowance in the private.

This was public; me trying wasn't enough
sitting on a fallen tree as if I was the one who
had fallen with the fog rolling in over the
choppy blue as it started to sprinkle.

But maybe those were my tears mimicking mist
or it was mist mimicking my tears, either way
ill-equipped for the weather the bright blue raincoat
tucked in the closet that no longer fit; outgrew it.

Blue on blue on blue till you hit the ocean floor, I
wasn't floored like the sand resting; these restless
legs conjured a wanderer out of me. My bench now
miles away, it was only self-proclaimed, anyways.

KNOWLEDGE
for Vincent van Gogh

Those sunflowers knew his depression even more than
he knew the back of his own hands that painted them.

He was probably trying to morph hope from his fraught
spirit into the tangible form; eleven paintings; they knew.

I know they were gently weeping when defaced by
protestors as his own hand once protested

against his own being that he cut off his own ear, and the
stars were a witness for that matter, dark matter.

Those depressions he didn't survive while I have made it. I
don't have survivor's guilt or maybe I do, and

just don't mess around with his paintings. Someone once
asked me at a poetry reading, "Are you a painter?" No.

I paint with words, but now treading cautiously on these
approaching syllables to be born writing slower

as this sadness becomes more real. If I could ask him just
one question, it would be: *Where is your safe place?*

POTENTIAL FOR THE LAST DANCE

Popping up unlike daisies, his memory never
hearing that voice. To hold the past in
one hand, and the future in another—now no
room for the present or to make a prayer;
ghostly footprints trampling my psyche
when doubts of demise arrived at different
points in time, those coordinates created
landed me here surrounded by the
felling of trees, the un-telling of history.

Tangible are my flesh and bones hanging
onto potential prancing through the barren
field while the wind twirls those white petals
ruffled unescaping the storm clouds rolling
in murky purple sky thunder proceeded by
flashes blinking my eyes, and lashing out at
the brokenness, burdened pixies trying to
take refuge covered in pollen having fallen
into the everchanging.

TO BREAK DREAMLAND

I broke dreamland in two no longer a dreamer
this land not of the free not tangible right out
of the gates no longer stands continental drift
drifting into sleep slipping survived over
10,000 nights never touched a mare even
with the claim these beasts are friendly.
I'm in a grassland star gazing to extract
the light, but they would vanish sky turned
pitch black a demon just flicked a switch
of the celestial bodies unable to pinpoint the
herd until they start sprinting towards me
hearing their hooves hitting the ground.
Jolted awake with my sheets soaked in sweat
despite the threat of death by horses I gravitated
towards those big eyes knowing they're wise
putting up posters on my bedroom walls.
I'm on an endless haunted merry-go-round
that was vandalized riding on the last
plastic horse standing with only one googly eye.
Unable to calculate the future, I subtracted
merry from go round so all that was left
was go round I tried to go round the earth
in search of meaning knowing the whole time
I must step away to see clearly in
order to birth new dreams.

LOST PRAYERS

Searching for three *Tums*

at midnight upset stomach

my mind cannot pray.

Look at a mirror

distance even though at arm's

length my reflection.

If only the cure

giving me *Tums* at midnight

alone in darkness.

A SAVIOR WHO COULDN'T SAVE
in memory of W.

Equipped with tarot cards, a priest with bright eyes
who tried to intervene to no avail couldn't light the
way out, and now I can barely remember his name
uttered just a few times almost sacrilegious to do so
seeing him once in a black and white photograph.

Supposedly smiling once a player on the minor league
baseball team buried secrets taken to the grave, I made
a promise to myself: *I will not end up like him.* Still
this life full of strife, to carry forward without my self-
proclaimed wishing "stone" I stole from her.

Composed and carved of an angel placed it in
my pocket of these jeans with a hole became holy
even though they were not what they started out to be.
Without him without ever seeing a yellow butterfly
yet they were born in my stomach. I shook my head.

The answer could have been finite or infinite
answers why this occurred, she was four before
I was born. No I'm not up in arms about it, but
that special day no longer wishing to witness
laughter, I walked the other way.

Out of my own 27th birthday party to skip
that "stone" in the lake near the place called
home unable to no longer possess a motionless
representation of flight—places in heaven
actually empty spaces.

68

THE THINGS THEY LEFT BEHIND

I
Adorned with tiny birds this cardboard tissue box:
three red, three green, one yellow on one side
next to a dead plant in a glass vase, probably branches
of a holly tree with red berries, but molded over sitting
in dirty water, rotting away. In that same nature, a
neglected book titled: *This Is How It Always Is*.

II
The cover a deep blue with stars and yellow wings
on a lone individual. To stop the bleeding, two tampons one
regular with an "R" white in color in a brown circle with
pink design and swirls packaging. A crinkled gold candy
wrapper, and a pink gel pen left unused, left untouched still
with the white protector plastic on the tip.

III
An empty plastic pink bottle once used for vaping in fact,
3,000 puffs of "Strawberry Ice Cream" written on the tube
on the back in faint white text barely legible: "WARNING:
THIS PRDOUCT CONTAINS NICOTINE. NICTOTINE
IS AN ADDICTIVE CHEMICAL." *This will expose you to
nicotine, birth defects.* A día de los muertos drawing.

IV
A skull with colorful tears, and flowers. A flower tucked
behind a dog's ear sketched in purple pen. An orbit gum
wrapper. A guidebook on the subject of the city San Jose
left near San Jose. A tag left behind for a jacket to take a
trek in: *Tek gear ultrasoft fleece warm, supports more-
sustainable cotton farming, stretch fabric.*

V

Two paint brushes wrapped in tin foil but only the heads
haphazardly—red handle, white handle. After unwrapped,
the paint brush bristles clean revealing a used folded up a
light blue rubber doctor glove. A gray sock inside out on
the floor. A stack of lined paper halfway in the plastic. 11
drawings on colorful rectangular papers on the wall.

VI

A drawing of a frog in red boots those high heels with a red
toadstool cap really a hat blushing with the text below "I
am what I create myself to be." Another says
"*BE HERE NOW*" above a sun but a tortured one with
charcoal eyes reminiscent of a face that died.
A sweatshirt with a vicious bull dog with teeth jutting out.

VII

It was the end of January when discovered an abandoned
Christmas themed gift bag with the text "Merry and
Bright", a tree, lights in the shapes of stars, acorns, and a
festive deep blue medium-small bow on the exterior
matching the cover *This Is How It Always Is*. Within, a
letter buried in the bag still in its envelope but opened.

VIII

At the bottom bright red shredded confetti missing a gift. A
card reads in all caps in green font floating above two
hearts overlapping pink and red, a stem with two leaves on
either side symmetrical: "*SENDING ALL MY LOVE*".
Inside black ink with neat handwriting except for an "a"
having it lowercase first then capitalized it, messed up "t".

IX
A compassionate note on the right side: *You've stayed strong and decided to get help which is something you should be so proud. Know you are cherished + loved by your family + friends. let's go hiking :) ♡ A* Pharmacy receipt. A hospital bill. On the left side of the card a poem transcribed carefully with care.

X
The things they left behind including this line:
""Hope" is a thing with feathers"

BUDDHA IN THE SHADOWS

Behind the statue

of the Buddha laced shadows

behind brambles lies.

Absence of light and

thereof a slender bird who

boasts tiny presence.

Screeching voice pecking

at the dead leaves trying to

sing its song trying to.

Find its way upward on

each slender branch half of

body in the sunlight.

ODE TO A PLATYPUS

A replica in the form of a children's
toy perhaps was how I first learned
of this creature's existence which is
deemed an unusual mammal who
lays eggs, and I'm still geographically
oblivious of where, and of why the
hysteria of the beanie-baby craze.

POETRY IS MY PRAYER

I was the one who got away from myself
running and running worn down countless
pairs of running shoes, all colors over
the years, if lined up this would create a rainbow
running from the rainbow, too, even though
"Somewhere Over The Rainbow" rang true
in childhood, running myself into the ground
self-hatred deemed the self as weak, laying
stomach down head to the side on the red
brick patio with the sun beating down on
my back, beads of sweat dripping down
while she'd rather want me to wear necklaces of
pretty beads, but not the rainbow, no and that day,
all alone the weight of the world too much
to hold up the sky trying not to die if I wasn't
a poet, I dare not want to think of what would've
happened to me, cannot be a self-fulfilling prophecy,
my moral duty to live, to survive, not up to being
another poet who falls, falls off the face of the
planet, expectations, I don't have the answers or
a beacon of light it's been bleak on and off like
the lighthouse flashing lights for over a decade
feeling weak, weeks keep going by people deem me
inspirational whereas I am sometimes scared of
these hands that can also work magic, a double-edged
sword, my purple pen is no sword a sword is not
a pen, and this leads me back to when.

28TH TRIP AROUND THE SUN

"the day, the sunset, oh ragged and bloody as a piece
of raw meat in the jaws of a golden carnivore"
—Diane Seuss, *frank:sonnets*

The light from the sun rising ray of reprieve
as the skin burned no need for candles nor
cake. This is much larger than flour, eggs, sugar,
combined forget the red dye I cannot be another
poet who falls. At age sixteen having entered the
children's psych ward unable to ward off
demons creeping in broad daylight.

If a sword was a pen, that would be double-edged.
Perhaps disadvantageous or perhaps advantageous
depending on the vantage point. Confined to that
small room even more so as I was given time-outs
from cursing at the nurses, sharing a room with
a suicidal kid, but you cannot out time or find the
sacred in those small spaces surveillanced.

Never had an attempt, but dwelled on it while too
many of my comrades have fallen without a
sword still this is not an actual war some say battle.
I wouldn't attach connotations from that field even
though this mind can do more than tricks, not pretty
magic, more like vomiting golden glitter. The light
shining too bright or not at all. Risk factors.

Yet I will never be a mathematician, but know my
birthday cake's circumference is 9 inches whereas
the sun's circumference is roughly 2,715,396 miles.
If only the sunset could be the onset of a cure which
begs the question that I try to avoid, and redirect attention.

Instead, I lassoed the sun, that carnivore preying
on the cattle that became the meats of yesterday.

To this day I hate that song "Yesterday" and stomp on
little beetles with my bare feet, juice, hate using the word
hate as I watched a sixteen-year-old release a golden
balloon letting go of the string up to the makeshift
heaven in the haze of a sky streaked red.

BIRTHDAY BLUES

I hear you, wishing to fight for
you to see the "we" in welding,
I wish to weld you a shield of any
type tangible or intangible, we need
each other not just a lone individual
with that magnificent shining sword.
I have fallen for you, I wish to gift
you an endless ladder to climb out
from this place headspace this strife
this life to the top of the world yet
the world is a like a sphere, but
still not quite.

The universal language you speak of,
perhaps is the ocean the water yet
to some the desert the sand dunes,
to me, universality is seeing past
someone's façade into their heartspace
their essence their art another trip
around the sun, and I'm blessed to have
met you, wish I could bedazzle your
spirit with glitter to let your spirit shine,
let your spirit breathe deeply, let the
rainbow prevail instead of sorrow
raining down your cheek like sweat
dripping like the wax of a dying candle.

The light and dark and dark and
light those shadows, birthday blues
I hear you, nowhere near in your shoes,
yes we do need that ladder to reach
for the stars yet your eyes, when they
twinkle with that shine, for poetry,
they are stars to me.

GLOW STICKS

She is asking me to wish upon something I cannot
see, to believe in there is another side and a way out, but
light pollution and pollution of light; yearning for
my eyes to ignite with the sheer amount of power
from the hands waving the countless neon glow sticks
(at the concert) but to amass this energy: effort and effort
I reiterate to her that I'm so tired and weary.

Yet she is leading me across as I'm barely hanging on, I
made a conscious choice to believe her belief in the beyond
and with one of my fingers grasping the edge of the
lifeboat, she said: "That's all you need, you have me."

That night equipped with my map and my compass, I
arrived at the exact coordinates on the crossroad of Hate
and Hope streets, and I gazed upwards to wish upon that
star that I cannot see, but all the while knowing that light
exists.

HAIKU TRAIN: RAILWAYS 3

poetry ignite
my ember my flame my fire
never extinguished

existentialism
may be the way live without
street signs spelling out

energy to moon
and back bursting with the blank
possibilities

bodies and bodies
not a hugger but hold my
hand help me feel safe

orange circle net
winning time over my mind
sad fades away

no need for balloons
in my mind's eye I fly far
from suffering now

MINE

moments upon moments built me
to be the person that I am today
trying to bloom despite the odds
relentless effort encouraged the
possibility of my future to shine
more brightly like my immortal
sunflower with its sixteen foot
legacy living on as I press on
with one foot in front of the other
despite heaviness of emotion while
holding faith seeds of sunflowers in
my right palm, ready.

YOURS

Across the grassy field all possible directions seemingly the
same as she walked away becoming a tiny dot on the
horizon with a red umbrella in her left hand to be
relieved from the relentless sun so tiny becoming
a pixel strolling away she twirls the red taking
my heart as she glanced back to get the last
words declaring: "You have the ocean."
this seemingly infinite source while
her and I our hours limited in this
plane of existence even though
we traveled to the beyond and
back now this disappearing
act, and when she faded
away it was as if I was
hit by a wave that
swept me off
my feet.

OURS

I

Knowing my tears were trapped, droplets not born into existence unlike me, she placed the tangible on top of the intangible performing the impossible lending a helping hand to me, allowing me to wrap my head around it while I had to wrap my writing hand with athletic tape to cover up injured blood vessels. Another joked , "You're a tree puncher, not a tree hugger" not seeing the reasons why I hit the trees not deserving of this damage so damn hard.

II

Deep sorrow grew downwards like the roots of the weeping willow tree then this tree no longer a tree instead with fragmented branches falling into the river becoming driftwood without making a splash whereas we got our feet wet into the unknown the answer became closer, together in such a finite and an infinite dose of time, I used to fear closeness, she, who saw all of me taught me these possibilities like the first pepper grown in outer-space.

III

She would twirl swirl her love, heat as I chopped up the jalapeños our time together timeless unlike a shooting star burning up my heart, she asked me: "What's wrong?" as she saw through the façade of this exterior of the outline of this body the outline of these eyes, it was her who saw the tears that were guarded for many years this connection of our heartspaces bridged together like a swirling of yellow butterflies going upward flying.

BUBBLES

This portal we entered then exited was like the
lifespan of a bubble—existence fleeting.

From the little orange plastic bottle, the heart-shaped
wand was twirled gently, and the solution blown through.

Bubbles born transporting kids to wonderland
who witness their beginning to their ending.

Faces most joyous at the finale whereas I wanted
to hold onto ours for eternity, two bubbles that merged.

This bond popped by a thorn on a rose bush, and
she knew my least favorite color was red.

Knowing I would get scared of my own hands
that too could draw red, not just the nurse drawing blood.

My defender unarmed while I never believed in angels
only demons yet she was my guardian angel in the flesh.

Our time together flew by with no easy solution, instead
of falling further, I took a turn and blew bubbles.

HER ORANGE CRAYON

The orange crayon made the setting
sun possible as he held on to the string
taking him upwards that was made possible
by the birth of creativity, outside the lines
as the string swayed as chaos ensued as the
orange crayon became smaller such force from
a small hand from the will of imagination.

WISHING

This shadow floating aimlessly across the blank
wall. Drawing a blank. On my first memory.

This puppet. My choice. A butterfly confined.
Not etched in. Missing bright colors and eyes.
I believed I was living in the shadows.

Of who I once was still after all that time
wanting to fly and to not die. My empty
heart at night still beating still pumping
blood. Woke up with a jolt.

Butterflies born in my stomach ready to burst.
They started rising to my chest. Knots. Now
caught in my throat not a net. Migration.
Upwards. This suffering trying to hold it
down when this needs to reach the outside.

To see the light. I threw up these butterflies
in the middle of the night. Illuminating this
room with me alone in bed like shooting stars.
These effervescent butterflies fluttering about.
I opened my palms. One perched on my
fingertip, and I made a wish

NEVER LET YOUR LIGHT FADE AWAY—KNOW YOU WILL GET THROUGH IT AND OUT OF IT.

In memoriam for the Poets before me who had fallen too soon—this is for you, too.

Out of respect for those special people in my life who: instilled in me the belief to hang on because life indeed is worth it, who told me to never give up on myself, and who made space for me, held me, and who continue to hold me in their heartspaces—together, we can persevere.

Sophia Falco is the author of *Farewell Clay Dove* (UnCollected Press, 2021) and of her award-winning chapbook *The Immortal Sunflower*. She is the winner of the Mirabai Prize for Poetry. Falco has over 40 poems published in various literary journals and magazines. In addition, she graduated *magna cum laude* with the highest honors in The Literature Department from the University of California, Santa Cruz. She is now a Master of Fine Arts Student for Poetry carrying out a Teaching Fellowship at Saint Mary's College of California on her way to make her dream career a reality to become a Professor.

Chronicles of Cosmic Chaos: In The Fourth Dimension continues Sophia Falco's poetic and psychic-spiritual quest to represent, figure forth, and express altered states of affect and moods of embodied-disembodied being. She goes on crossing slings and arrows of "cosmic chaos" as entrance into trances, tropes, and traces of a "fourth dimension." In this her third book, the forms have become more compressed, adjudications of meaning more secure as line, stanza, form. Sophia is on a poetic journey and takes the reader into the sacred heart of bipolar transformation and migration: herein younger self, future self, and present self collide and collude into a plot of survivance, radiance, love, and life wisdom.

—**Rob Sean Wilson**, author of *When the Nikita Moon Rose* and *Waking in Seoul*

"Sophia Falco's poems are luminous, rich paths of acceptance. Generous in their attention to detail, they are transformative in their celebrations of the local, the neighbor, the details that make each person unique."

—**Juliana Spahr**, author of *This Connection of Everyone with Lungs*

The poems in *Chronicles of Cosmic Chaos* are deeply contemplative. They reach back into memory to reveal a fleeting image, simple yet profound, or perhaps a quiet gesture, a shared moment of joy or grief.

—**Aaron Lelito**, Editor in Chief of *Wild Roof Journal*

"Sophia's poems are wonderfully specific and personal. They contain unexpected details that color a solitary moment or spark a memory. From this, themes of love and suffering, connection and impermanence emerge. It's a beautiful collection."

—**Maya Highland**, Editor of *The Closed Eye Open*

Grab ahold of Sophia's hand as she leads you into the fourth dimension; a place filled with heartache, contrast, darkness, and light. Falco's heartfelt poetry will spin you into a stunning expanse of comic chaos.

—Tiny Seed Literary Journal

Within the "Chaos," control and contradiction define Sophia Falco's newest volume of poems. This mature work showcases her deliberate craft as she coaxes memories and impressions into poetic form, allowing each emotion to dictate shape and style, affirming, "yes, a method / to this madness" in a "World Backwards." This surprising variety captures and mimics the complexity of our thoughts and the intimate relationships that are at the heart of this work–the expectations, longing, disappointments, and reverence–the very pulse of humanity in all of its delight and pain. On full display is her characteristic marriage of opposites. Childlike fantasy colors the grips of despair. Hope refuses to be drowned. And as we enter the fourth dimension with her, time is suspended, allowing us to hold up and examine more than one "blue green marble" that is "more than just a marble" and see "that light exists."

—**Allison Herman,** Professor of English at Foothill College

ACKNOWLEDGEMENTS

"Spider Legs" *Lighthouse Weekly*

"To Break Dreamland" *Wild Roof Journal*

"Yours" *The Closed Eye Open* & Featured Selection

"Ours" *The Closed Eye Open*

"Tiger For The Nth Time" *Indolent Books*

"Spectator" *The AutoEthnographer*

"Poetry Is My Prayer" *The AutoEthnographer*

"Birthday Blues" *The AutoEthnographer*

"28th Trip Around The Sun" *Moonstone Press, 26ᵗʰ Annual Poetry Ink* Anthology

"Birdie Hop" *The Raw Art Review*

"Claws" *The Raw Art Review*

"A Trip To Jolene's" *Out Loud: An LGBTQ Literary and Art* Anthology; Read or Green Books

"Beyond The Beyond" *International Bipolar Foundation*

"The First Time" *International Bipolar Foundation*

"Haiku Train: Railways" *International Bipolar Foundation*

"Glow Sticks" *International Bipolar Foundation*

www.ingramcontent.com/pod-product-compliance
Lightning Source LLC
Chambersburg PA
CBHW022035090426
42741CB0000 7B/1069